The
Turtle Club
Handbook

JAMES HATCHER

ISBN-13: 978-1497528352
ISBN-10: 1497528356

Available from Amazon.com, CreateSpace.com,
and other retail outlets

www.CreateSpace.com/4743201

Printed by CreateSpace, Charleston SC
An Amazon.com Company

THIS HANDBOOK BELONGS TO

_____

NAME

_____

PHONE

_____

EMAIL

_____

POND OR TURTLE CLUB

_____

LOCATION

DEDICATION

This book is dedicated to all those Turtles out there,
of any brand, who have promised to further the cause of
Turtlism and to willingly stick their neck out for a friend in need.

CONTENTS

ACKNOWLEDGMENTS

We wish to acknowledge those crazy WWII Bomber Pilots and all those who followed after them aiding in the continuation and preservation down through the decades of that sublime informal and unorganized band of Brothers and Sisters, commonly referred to by many brands, but bound together in fraternalism as a unique part of

THE ANCIENT AND HONORABLE ORDER OF TURTLES

1 TURTLE BASICS

Are You a Turtle? Many members of America's great fraternal organizations, such as the Shriners, Masons, Elks, and American Legionnaires, are familiar with that age-old query, "Are you a Turtle?" Sometimes, one sees a green-shelled turtle lapel pin or tie tack, or even an auto decal with a grinning turtle asking the same question. But what or who are the Turtles, you ask?

Quite simply, the Turtles are a drinking fraternity that exists in the United States of America as a fun-and-honor group usually within the local lodge or post, sort of a side degree. It traces its honorable origins back to the Second World War, on January 12, 1943 in an English pub, when a group of fighter pilots formed a semisecret drinking fraternity among its squadron's members, and put prospective candidates for membership through a mock initiation.

Legend of the Turtle

Once upon a time, many years ago there was a man who was of good and noble character; without a trace of impurity in his thoughts. Unfortunately, all about him he saw persons with vulgar minds unable to think of anything, except in sexual terms. He bemoaned his inability to find others with a similar high mindedness, to his own. Like a turtle, he retreated into his shell. Then one day, while partaking of a pint of ale (for purely medicinal purposes of course),

1

he realized that there must be others like him. Forced into bars, and saloons; imbibing alcohol as a balm for the ills inflicted by obscene and vulgar persons. He resolved to locate all the other pure minded individuals that he could, even if this meant spending his every waking hour crawling from one bar to the next. This was the beginning of the Turtles. He embarked upon this quest with vigor and determination, but, since he was a man of limited means, quickly ran out of money. Then one day, he got a tip on a horse running at long odds at the local track. The problem was that he had no money left with which to gamble. So, in desperation he wagered his last and most prized possession a donkey which he had raised from birth. Now this donkey was a particularly gentle and temperate animal, with a loving disposition. To lose his donkey would have been devastating, and yet what choice was there if the quest was to continue? Fortunately, he won the wager, and with the money was able to continue in his search for many more years, and begin the association of Turtles we know today.

History of the Order

The late Captain Hugh P. McGowan, U.S. Army Air Corps/U.S. Air Force Reserve (Ret.), he and several pilots of the U.S. Army Air Corps 8th Air Force founded the Ancient and Honorable Order of Turtles in an officers' club while stationed in England during the Second World War: "We were flying daytime bombing missions over Hitler's Third Reich. We just wanted a little fun. We had seen a sign showing that the 'Ancient Order of Foresters' and the 'Royal Antediluvian Order of Buffalos' would meet in the local pub, so I devised the name 'Ancient and Honorable Order of Turtles' for the fun of it. It was not meant to be serious; it had no constitution or by-laws, and was a relief from the horrors and dangers we saw every day on our missions. It spread after the War through the VFW and American Legion posts, and eventually, to colleges and even to the high schools of the U.S.A."

Now, some Turtle history about an astronaut was asked the question, "Are you a Turtle?" by ground control, Wally Schirra who was asked:

"Just a minute, Wally. Let's see. Oh, it's a little message to Deke Slayton. A little bit closer Wally. Kind of looks like something about - 'Are you a, are you a --'" Schirra acknowledged, "That's right." CAPCOM continued, "Looks like it says, 'Are you a turtle, Deke Slayton?'"

Schirra confirmed, "That's right." Eisele added, "You get an A for reading today Jack." Swigert continued, "Here comes another one. Walt, oh, that-a-way, that's the way to turn it. It says, 'Paul Haney, are you a turtle?'" Cunningham radioed, "You'll get a gold star. Perfect score!" Swigert reported, "And there is no reply from Paul Haney there." Cunningham asked, "You mean he's speechless?"

A short while later, CAPCOM Cernan informed Schirra, "Wally, this is Gene. Deke just called in, and we've got your answer, and we've got it recorded for you return." Schirra acknowledged, "Roger. Real fine."

Shortly thereafter, Schirra asked CAPCOM Swigert, "Have you got Haney's answer yet?" Swigert replied, "No, Haney's isn't talking, Wally." Swigert then added, "Somebody tells me he isn't talking, but just buying." A pleased Schirra responded, "He is buying. Thank you very much. Very good." This exchange about turtles was a reference to the notorious Turtle's Club drinking club of which Wally Schirra held the title of a Grand Potentate. During Schirra's Mercury flight Deke Slayton had radioed up to Schirra, asking Schirra if he was a turtle.

The Challenge and Correct Response

The proper response for a member of the Turtle's Club to give when challenged by another Turtle member could be misconstrued if taken out of context. The expectation is that every Turtle has in their possession a donkey. So the proper Turtle response is, "You bet your sweet ass I am." If a Turtle member fails to give the appropriate response, then they owe a drink to the turtle asking the question.

Turtle Creed

Turtles are bright eyed, bushy tailed fearless & unafraid folks with a fighter pilot attitude. They think clean, have fun a lot, & recognize the fact that you never get any place worthwhile in life unless you stick your neck out.

The Grip of the Order

The Grip or secret handshake of the Turtle Club is done as follows:

Place the middle and index fingers against the wrist of the other Turtle. Press the fingers gently against the wrist, as they do the same to your wrist. This is to feel the alcohol pulsing through each other's veins!

The Grand Hailing Sign

The Grand Hailing Sign of the Turtle Club is done as follows:

Place your right hand level with your chest, closed in a fist with the thumb pointing outwards. Cover the right hand with your left hand, allowing the right thumb to stick out. See the noble Turtle, sticking his head from his shell for a friend in need.

Password

Y.B.Y.S.A.I.A / or buy a drink

Turtle Call

Bloop! Bloop!

2 STARTING YOUR OWN POND

Where do Turtles Meet? On the Pond

For those Turtles who desire a more formal organization, there is the Pond.

A Pond (Chapter) is a local club of Turtles, who meet together occasionally, or regularly, to have fun and do good works. A pond may be started by at least three members, who are Turtles:

Pond Officers and their Responsibilities

For charitable purposes, the required three officers would be the Master Turtle, Turtle Secretary, and Turtle Treasurer. For social purposes, the three required officers would be the Master Turtle, Senior and Junior Turtles.

Master Turtle (MT) – Presides over the Pond.

Senior Turtle (ST) – Assists in the opening of the Pond in the absence of the Master Turtle.

Junior Turtle (JT) – Assist in opening the Pond in the absence of Master Turtle and Senior Snapper.

Senior Conductor Turtle (SCT) – To conduct the Candidates on their journey.

Junior Conductor Turtle (JCT) – To conduct and assist in the work of the Pond.

Turtle Secretary (TSecy) – To keep the minutes and records of the Pond.

Turtle Treasurer (TTr) – To keep track of pond monies and charitable donations.

Turtle Marshal (TMar) – To keep the peace of the Pond.

Turtle Sentinel (TSen) – To guard within the Pond door.

Turtle Warder (TW) – To guard within the Pond door.

Turtle Tyler (TT) – To guard without the Pond door.

Turtle Chaplain – Render prayer.

Of course, you will need a place to meet. This can be a fraternal hall or lodge, a neighborhood bar and grill, or your own home. It really doesn't matter, as long as there is fun, friendship and the swamp water of your choice.

3 TURTLE CLUB INITIATION

The Ancient and Honorable Order of Turtles (WWII Bomber Pilots) and the International Association of Turtles (Masonic Order)

The original initiation was quite simple. It consisted of the candidate being asked four questions. As all members are of clean mind to become an official Turtle the person must solve the following riddles with clean-minded correct answers, called the Sublime Test of the Four Questions:

1. What is it a man can do standing up, a woman sitting down, and a dog on three legs? *Shake Hands*

2. What is it that a cow has four of and woman has only two of? *Legs*

3. What is a four letter word ending in 'k' that means the same as intercourse? *Talk*

4. What is it on a man that is round, hard, and sticks so far out of his pajamas that you can hang a hat on it? *His Head*

The Order was not meant to be serious, as it had no constitution or by-laws, no formal applications for membership, no dues or fees, and a simple initiation ritual.

After the completion of The Interrogation, and all of The Four Sublime Questions are presented and answered by the candidate, the presiding officer asks all the Turtles present to vote on whether the candidate should be admitted into their ranks as a Brother or Sister Turtle. The Turtles step aside from the candidate and hold a conclave. There is much grumbling and whispering in the circle, and finally, they agree to admit the candidate.

The circle is re-formed around the candidate, and they are advised by the presiding officer:

"Candidate, you have been found worthy and well-qualified for membership in our Order. By the authority invested in me by the Ancient and Honorable Order of Turtles, I shall now invest you with the sign, grip, and passwords of the Order, which you shall divulge to no one except duly initiated Turtles. As a Brother (or Sister) Turtle, know ye that all Turtles are your brethren. When asked the password by a Brother or Sister Turtle, and you fail to give the proper response in its entirety, you shall forfeit to that Turtle a beverage of their choice. If you ask a Brother or Sister Turtle the password, and they fail to give you the password in its entirety, they shall forfeit to you a beverage of your choice. As a new Brother (or Sister) Turtle, I welcome you into the Order, and by this sign, grip, and password, identify yourself to each Brother and Sister in this circle."

The new Brother or Sister Turtle then goes around the circle of new friends, and gives the sign, handclasp and password to each. The next candidate is then called upon to join, and the procedure is commenced once again.

The Modern Branches of the Order

Over the decades since the second world war, the Order has developed many branches under various names, and the ritual of gaining membership expanded.

The questions have expanded, remaining in the spirit of the original ones, but still requiring that only four be asked to the candidate. Here is an incomplete list of modern questions that one may choose to ask a candidate, if not sticking to the original four:

1. What does a woman do sitting down; that a man does standing up, that a dog does on three legs? *Shake hands*

2. What word begins with an F and ends with a UCK? *Firetruck*

3. What's hairy, hard and sticks out of a man's pajamas at night? *His head*

4. What four letter word, ending in K, represents intercourse between a man and a women? *Talk*

5. What is it that a cow has four of and a woman only two? *Legs*

6. What goes in hard but comes out soft and wet? *Gum*

7. What does a dog do that a man steps in? *Pants*

8. What can you find in a man's pants that is about six inches long, has a head on it, and that women love so much they often blow? *A twenty dollar bill*

9. Name five words that are each four letters long, end in u-n-t, one of which is a word for a woman? *Aunt*

10. What four letter word begins with f and ends with k, and if you can't get one you can use your hands? *Fork*

11. What is hard, six inches long, has two nuts, and can make a girl fat? *Almond Joy*

12. What four-letter word ends in i-t and is found on the bottom of birdcages? *Grit*

13. What is it that all men have one of; that is longer on some men than others, that the Pope doesn't use, and that a man gives to his wife after they're married *his last name*

14. What is it on a man that gets very large when he is excited? *his pupils*

15. What is long, round, wet and full of sea men? *A Submarine*

16. What starts with a "C" and ends with a "T", is hairy, oval, delicious and contains thin whitish liquid? *Coconut*

17. I am a protrusion that comes in many sizes. When I'm not well, I drip. When you blow me, you feel good. What am I? *A Nose*

18. I'm spread before I'm eaten. Your tongue gets me off. People sometimes lick my nuts. What am I? *Peanut Butter*

19. I assist an erection. Sometimes big balls hang from me. I'm called a big swinger. What am I? *A Crane*

20. Over 1,000 people went down on me. I wasn't a maiden for long. A big hard thing ripped me open. What am I? *The Titanic*

21. You stick your poles inside me. You tie me down to get me up. I get wet before you do. What am I? *A Tent*

22. When I go in I cause pain. I cause you to spit and ask you not to swallow. I can fill your hole. What am I? *A Dentist*

23. A finger goes in me. You fiddle with me when you're bored. The best man always has me first. What am I? *A Wedding Ring*

24. All day long, it's in and out. I discharge loads from my shaft. Both men and women go down on me. What am I? *An Elevator*

25. If I miss, I hit your bush. It's my job to stuff your box. When I come, it's news. What am I? *A Newspaper Boy*

26. I offer Protection. I get the finger ten times. You use your

fingers to get me off. What am I? *A Glove*

27. I have a stiff shaft. My tip penetrates. I come with a quiver. What am I? *An Arrow*

28. My business is briefs. I am a cunning linguist. I plead and plead for it. What am I? *An Attorney*

29. I go in hard. I come out soft. You blow me hard. What am I? *Chewing Gum*

A Modern Masonic-Styled Turtle Initiation Ritual

Adapted from the website ancientturtleorder.webs.com by a group under the name of the Ancient and Honorable Order of the Turtle.

(* denotes gavel raps)

Chapter Opening

MT: ** Snappers please come together as turtles. Officers please take your seats in the four corners. Senior Snapper, are you sure all present are turtles?

ST: Yes, Master Turtle all present are Brother/sister turtles.

(OR)

ST: Master Turtle I do not know and will ascertain the worthiness of the turtles gathered. (ST will ask the brother/sister in a low voice RUAT? With a return of YBYSAIA! Those without the pass will be asked to wait at the bar with patience so they can be recommended for membership.)

MT: Brother/sister Senior Turtle RUAT?

ST: YBYSAIA!

MT: What induced you to become a turtle?

ST: In order I might come out of my shell.

MT: Where were you made a turtle?

ST: In a chapter of turtles.

MT: What number constitutes a chapter of turtles?

ST: Seven or more consisting of Master Turtle, Senior and Junior Turtle, Senior and Junior Conductor turtle, Marshall Turtle.

MT: Where is the place of the Senior and Junior Conductor turtles?

ST: At the right side of the table.

MT: SCT why on the right side of the table?

SCT: To see that mugs are frosty foamy and full.

MT: Where is the place of the Junior turtle?

SCT: At the left side of the table.

MT: JT why at the left side of the table?

JT: To make sure that drinks are ordered promptly.

MT: Where is the place of the Senior Turtle?

JT: At the end of the table.

MT: ST why at the end of the table?

ST: To make sure that all tabs are paid by the end of the night.

MT: Where is the place of the Chapter President?

ST: At the head of the table.

MT: Why at the head?

ST: To observe the pleasure of the turtles gathered and to make sure that all present are part of the group.

MT: It is my order that this chapter of turtles now be open. Turtles please remember that a turtle is never vulgar, always cheerful, and always willing to stick his/her neck out for a fellow turtle.

MT: ** Turtles please join me in the opening toast. Weather Turtles Near, Weather Turtles Far, you will find turtles at their favorite bars.

MT: Turtles where do we meet?

ALL: On the pond

MT: *

Turtle Initiation Ceremony

The Turtles approach the prospective candidate and solemnly ask him (or her);

SCT: Do you wish to join the ancient & honorable fraternal order of Turtles?"

If the candidate agrees to join the Turtles, they are taken to a side room or private area where the initiation can be conducted in relative privacy....if background music is being played that substitutes as a private area. Phone initiations are allowed too.

The candidate is advised that:

SCT: You are about to join an honorable drinking fraternity composed of ladies and gentlemen of the highest morals and good character, ladies and gentlemen who are never vulgar. It

is assumed by the Turtles that you the candidate also own a donkey of a sweet and kindly disposition. Do you have a Donkey?

MT: *** Fellow Turtles, it has come to my attention that Brother/Sister_____ wishes to become a turtle. Turtles will you please form the circle of friendship. *(All Turtles form a circle around with the officers at the four corners. Candidate is left outside circle only to hear mumbles and whispers)*

MT: Brother/Sister _____ after much deliberation it has been unanimously agreed that you may join the turtle lodge.

MT: Brother/Sister _____ please make your way to the center of the circle with a full drink in hand.

ST: You will be asked a series of four riddles the answers to are NEVER vulgar; the wrong answer will result in a penalty of drinking a quarter of your drink. The correct will result in us drinking a quarter of ours. Either way it is a win-win situation.

Candidate steps to the center of the circle and is asked questions

SCT asks questions and receives answers.

* *All are seated unless there is another candidate then the first candidate will join the circle and the process will repeat***

SCT: I will now explain to you the story of the turtles.

…Once upon a time, many years ago there was a man who was of good and noble character; without a trace of impurity in his thoughts. Unfortunately all about him he saw persons with vulgar minds unable to think of anything, except in sexual terms. He bemoaned his inability to find others with a similar high- mindedness, to his own. Like a turtle, he retreated into his shell. Then one day, while partaking of a pint of ale (for purely medicinal purposes of course), he realized that there must be others like him. Forced into bars, and saloons;

imbibing alcohol as a balm for the ills inflicted by obscene and vulgar persons. He resolved to locate all the other pure minded individuals that he could, even if this meant spending his every waking hour crawling from one bar to the next. This was the beginning of the Turtles. He embarked upon this quest with vigor and determination, but, since he was a man of limited means, quickly ran out of money. Then one day, he got a tip on a horse running at long odds at the local track. The problem was that he had no money left with which to gamble. So, in desperation he wagered his last and most prized possession a donkey which he had raised from birth. Now this donkey was a particularly gentle and temperate animal, with a loving disposition. To lose his donkey would have been devastating, and yet what choice was there if the quest was to continue? Fortunately, he won the wager, and with the money was able to continue in his search for many more years, and begin the association of Turtles we know today. And so, to commemorate this event, all members of this esteemed organization when asked, "Are You a Turtle?", must respond immediately without hesitation or fear of embarrassment, in a voice as loud and clear as the voice of the questioner: "You bet your sweet ass, I am"! Failure to do so at any time, will be penalized by having to buy a beer for everyone close enough to have heard the original question.

ST: I will now impart on you the due guard and grip of a turtle. This is the due guard of a turtle it alludes to a turtle coming out of his shell and sticking his neck out for a fellow turtle. This is the grip of a turtle with the two fingers extended so that you may feel not only the alcohol but friendship flowing through your companion's veins.

SCT: We will now explain to you the Working Tools of the Imperial Turtle.

...Behold the stirring stick and bottle opener; these are essential working tools of the Imperial Turtle. The stirring stick teaches us to mix up life a little bit, not to get stuck in the same boring routine of having the same drink day after day use this tool wisely and have fun. The bottle opener teaches us that no matter what difficulties are presented to us in life there is always a way break through and enjoy its rewards. The Jigger is the emblem of the Senior and Junior Turtles and teaches us about drinking within our means, some of us can drink more some of use less, let us drink to within our limits. The Muddler, is the emblem of the Senior and Junior Conductor Turtles and is that special tools that reminds us that we all come from many places and backgrounds, and we blend ourselves with each other and become one greater Turtle.

JT: Amongst these working tools you will find the Beer Mug, Martini Glass, and Shot glass; these are to teach us that sublime principle: "to each their own." Every Turtle has his or her personal likes and dislikes and that we as Imperial Turtles, should respect that.

ST: As stated before you will find the Bartenders Book, is a special text to all Imperial Turtles, as it shows us all the different ways to cure the ill effects of life. It teaches us how to use your medicinal liquors wisely, perfecting our designs and creations. Go forth and find others who read this special text because they will be of equal high mindedness and class.

MT: In my hand you will find the most important working tool of the Imperial Turtle, the cocktail shaker. Even with all the other tools it is impossible to mix a perfect drink without this glorious device, in the words of the great James Bond all good drinks are shaken…not stirred.

All Turtles: Brothers/Sisters (pointing at the new initiates) RUAT?

Candidates: YBYSAIA/or buying a drink.

Chapter Closing

MT: Brother/sister Senior Turtle RUAT?

ST: YBYSAIA!

MT: What induced you to become a turtle?

ST: In order I might come out of my shell.

MT: Where were you made a turtle?

ST: In a chapter of turtles.

MT: What number constitutes a chapter of turtles?

ST: Six or more consisting of Master Turtle, Senior and Junior Turtle, Senior and Junior Conductor turtle

MT: Where is the place of the Senior and Junior Conductor turtles?

ST: At the right side of the table.

MT: SCT why on the right side of the table?

SCT: To see that mugs are frosty foamy and full.

MT: Where is the place of the Junior turtle?

SCT: At the left side of the table.

MT: JT why at the left side of the table?

JT: To make sure that drinks are ordered promptly.

MT: Where is the place of the Senior Turtle?

JT: At the end of the table.

MT: ST why at the end of the table?

ST: To make sure that all tabs are paid by the end of the night.

MT: Where is the place of the Chapter President?

ST: At the head of the table.

MT: Why at the head?

ST: To observe the pleasure of the turtles gathered and to make sure that all present are part of the group.

MT: ** Turtles please join me in the closing toast.

...Whether Turtles Near, Whether Turtles Far, you will find turtles at their favorite bars. May we come together as friends and leave with only the wind to our Backs

MT: Turtles how do we depart?

ALL: On the shell

MT: *

4 DEGREES OF THE ORDER

There are seven (7) ancient Turtle degrees. They are:

Candidate – a person invited to become a Turtle;

Turtle – a Brother or Sister member duly initiated into the Order;

Snapping Turtle – A Brother or Sister Turtle who has personally initiated 25 new Turtles;

Grand Snapping Turtle – A Brother or Sister Turtle who has initiated 50 or more Turtles;

Imperial Turtle – A Brother or Sister Turtle who has initiated 100 or more Turtles;

Past Imperial Turtle – A Brother or Sister who has initiated at least 150 new Turtles into the Order;

Master Imperial Turtle – A Brother or Sister who has initiated at least 500 new Turtles into the Order.

To progress through the different degrees, all that is required is that you personally initiate new Turtles into the Order. This can be informally or formally, as there are no official "rules" for initiation.

Heck, there really are no for anything in the Order, other than you MUST bring in new members and have fun!

If you go the formal route for your particular Pond, then you may wish to establish a color-coded rank recognition program. One way to do that is for each member to purchase a Green Fez (traditional Moroccan hat with tassel). These can be purchased online for around $20.00 and include the tassel. Or, you could use green ball caps. Shoot, you can even make your own tassels inexpensively with embrordery thread. An R U A TURTLE patch or pin can be affixed to the front of the fez or cap.

The proposed system for Turtle Members could be as follows:

Turtle – Green Fez with Green Tassel
Snapping Turtle – Green Fez with White Tassel
Grand Snapping Turtle – Green Fez with Gold Tassel
Imperial Turtle – Green Fez with Black Tassel
Past Imperial Turtle – Green Fez with Red Tassel
Master Imperial Turtle – Green Fez with Purple Tassel

And for Pond Officers:

Past Master Turtle – Red Fez
Current Master Turtle – White Fez
Current Pond Officer – Black Fez

It is highly suggested that you do not use a maroon fez, as the Moroccan turtles may get offended. There are too few ponds in Morocco, and we do not want to abuse the national privilege of these water-deprived turtles...not to mention those boys over at the Shrine.

The following pages will allow you to record your progress through the Degrees and travels across the ponds of our Great Society.

Snapping Turtle Degree

1	Name		Date
	❏ In Person ❏ By Phone ❏ By Email/Online		Location
2	Name		Date
	❏ In Person ❏ By Phone ❏ By Email/Online		Location
3	Name		Date
	❏ In Person ❏ By Phone ❏ By Email/Online		Location
4	Name		Date
	❏ In Person ❏ By Phone ❏ By Email/Online		Location
5	Name		Date
	❏ In Person ❏ By Phone ❏ By Email/Online		Location
6	Name		Date
	❏ In Person ❏ By Phone ❏ By Email/Online		Location

7	Name	Date
❑ In Person ❑ By Phone ❑ By Email/Online		Location
8	Name	Date
❑ In Person ❑ By Phone ❑ By Email/Online		Location
9	Name	Date
❑ In Person ❑ By Phone ❑ By Email/Online		Location
10	Name	Date
❑ In Person ❑ By Phone ❑ By Email/Online		Location
11	Name	Date
❑ In Person ❑ By Phone ❑ By Email/Online		Location
12	Name	Date
❑ In Person ❑ By Phone ❑ By Email/Online		Location
13	Name	Date
❑ In Person ❑ By Phone ❑ By Email/Online		Location
14	Name	Date
❑ In Person ❑ By Phone ❑ By Email/Online		Location

15	Name	Date
❏ In Person ❏ By Phone ❏ By Email/Online		Location
16	Name	Date
❏ In Person ❏ By Phone ❏ By Email/Online		Location
17	Name	Date
❏ In Person ❏ By Phone ❏ By Email/Online		Location
18	Name	Date
❏ In Person ❏ By Phone ❏ By Email/Online		Location
19	Name	Date
❏ In Person ❏ By Phone ❏ By Email/Online		Location
20	Name	Date
❏ In Person ❏ By Phone ❏ By Email/Online		Location
21	Name	Date
❏ In Person ❏ By Phone ❏ By Email/Online		Location
22	Name	Date
❏ In Person ❏ By Phone ❏ By Email/Online		Location

23	Name		Date
	❏ In Person ❏ By Phone ❏ By Email/Online		Location
24	Name		Date
	❏ In Person ❏ By Phone ❏ By Email/Online		Location
25	Name		Date
	❏ In Person ❏ By Phone ❏ By Email/Online		Location

Congratulations!
You are now a Snapping Turtle!

Grand Snapping Turtle Degree

26	Name	Date
❏ In Person ❏ By Phone ❏ By Email/Online		Location
27	Name	Date
❏ In Person ❏ By Phone ❏ By Email/Online		Location
28	Name	Date
❏ In Person ❏ By Phone ❏ By Email/Online		Location
29	Name	Date
❏ In Person ❏ By Phone ❏ By Email/Online		Location
30	Name	Date
❏ In Person ❏ By Phone ❏ By Email/Online		Location
31	Name	Date
❏ In Person ❏ By Phone ❏ By Email/Online		Location

32	Name	Date
	❑ In Person ❑ By Phone ❑ By Email/Online	Location
33	Name	Date
	❑ In Person ❑ By Phone ❑ By Email/Online	Location
34	Name	Date
	❑ In Person ❑ By Phone ❑ By Email/Online	Location
35	Name	Date
	❑ In Person ❑ By Phone ❑ By Email/Online	Location
36	Name	Date
	❑ In Person ❑ By Phone ❑ By Email/Online	Location
37	Name	Date
	❑ In Person ❑ By Phone ❑ By Email/Online	Location
38	Name	Date
	❑ In Person ❑ By Phone ❑ By Email/Online	Location
39	Name	Date
	❑ In Person ❑ By Phone ❑ By Email/Online	Location

40	Name		Date
	❏ In Person ❏ By Phone ❏ By Email/Online		Location
41	Name		Date
	❏ In Person ❏ By Phone ❏ By Email/Online		Location
42	Name		Date
	❏ In Person ❏ By Phone ❏ By Email/Online		Location
43	Name		Date
	❏ In Person ❏ By Phone ❏ By Email/Online		Location
44	Name		Date
	❏ In Person ❏ By Phone ❏ By Email/Online		Location
45	Name		Date
	❏ In Person ❏ By Phone ❏ By Email/Online		Location
46	Name		Date
	❏ In Person ❏ By Phone ❏ By Email/Online		Location
47	Name		Date
	❏ In Person ❏ By Phone ❏ By Email/Online		Location

48	Name	Date
	❑ In Person ❑ By Phone ❑ By Email/Online	Location
49	Name	Date
	❑ In Person ❑ By Phone ❑ By Email/Online	Location
50	Name	Date
	❑ In Person ❑ By Phone ❑ By Email/Online	Location

Congratulations!
You are now a Grand Snapping Turtle!

Imperial Turtle Degree

51	Name		Date
	❑ In Person ❑ By Phone ❑ By Email/Online		Location
52	Name		Date
	❑ In Person ❑ By Phone ❑ By Email/Online		Location
53	Name		Date
	❑ In Person ❑ By Phone ❑ By Email/Online		Location
54	Name		Date
	❑ In Person ❑ By Phone ❑ By Email/Online		Location
55	Name		Date
	❑ In Person ❑ By Phone ❑ By Email/Online		Location
56	Name		Date
	❑ In Person ❑ By Phone ❑ By Email/Online		Location

57	Name	Date
	❑ In Person ❑ By Phone ❑ By Email/Online	Location
58	Name	Date
	❑ In Person ❑ By Phone ❑ By Email/Online	Location
59	Name	Date
	❑ In Person ❑ By Phone ❑ By Email/Online	Location
60	Name	Date
	❑ In Person ❑ By Phone ❑ By Email/Online	Location
61	Name	Date
	❑ In Person ❑ By Phone ❑ By Email/Online	Location
62	Name	Date
	❑ In Person ❑ By Phone ❑ By Email/Online	Location
63	Name	Date
	❑ In Person ❑ By Phone ❑ By Email/Online	Location
64	Name	Date
	❑ In Person ❑ By Phone ❑ By Email/Online	Location

65	Name	Date
❑ In Person ❑ By Phone ❑ By Email/Online		Location
66	Name	Date
❑ In Person ❑ By Phone ❑ By Email/Online		Location
67	Name	Date
❑ In Person ❑ By Phone ❑ By Email/Online		Location
68	Name	Date
❑ In Person ❑ By Phone ❑ By Email/Online		Location
69	Name	Date
❑ In Person ❑ By Phone ❑ By Email/Online		Location
70	Name	Date
❑ In Person ❑ By Phone ❑ By Email/Online		Location
71	Name	Date
❑ In Person ❑ By Phone ❑ By Email/Online		Location
72	Name	Date
❑ In Person ❑ By Phone ❑ By Email/Online		Location

73	Name	Date
	❑ In Person ❑ By Phone ❑ By Email/Online	Location
74	Name	Date
	❑ In Person ❑ By Phone ❑ By Email/Online	Location
75	Name	Date
	❑ In Person ❑ By Phone ❑ By Email/Online	Location
76	Name	Date
	❑ In Person ❑ By Phone ❑ By Email/Online	Location
77	Name	Date
	❑ In Person ❑ By Phone ❑ By Email/Online	Location
78	Name	Date
	❑ In Person ❑ By Phone ❑ By Email/Online	Location
79	Name	Date
	❑ In Person ❑ By Phone ❑ By Email/Online	Location
80	Name	Date
	❑ In Person ❑ By Phone ❑ By Email/Online	Location

81	Name	Date
	❑ In Person ❑ By Phone ❑ By Email/Online	Location
82	Name	Date
	❑ In Person ❑ By Phone ❑ By Email/Online	Location
83	Name	Date
	❑ In Person ❑ By Phone ❑ By Email/Online	Location
84	Name	Date
	❑ In Person ❑ By Phone ❑ By Email/Online	Location
85	Name	Date
	❑ In Person ❑ By Phone ❑ By Email/Online	Location
86	Name	Date
	❑ In Person ❑ By Phone ❑ By Email/Online	Location
87	Name	Date
	❑ In Person ❑ By Phone ❑ By Email/Online	Location
88	Name	Date
	❑ In Person ❑ By Phone ❑ By Email/Online	Location

89	Name	Date
❑ In Person ❑ By Phone ❑ By Email/Online		Location
90	Name	Date
❑ In Person ❑ By Phone ❑ By Email/Online		Location
91	Name	Date
❑ In Person ❑ By Phone ❑ By Email/Online		Location
92	Name	Date
❑ In Person ❑ By Phone ❑ By Email/Online		Location
93	Name	Date
❑ In Person ❑ By Phone ❑ By Email/Online		Location
94	Name	Date
❑ In Person ❑ By Phone ❑ By Email/Online		Location
95	Name	Date
❑ In Person ❑ By Phone ❑ By Email/Online		Location
96	Name	Date
❑ In Person ❑ By Phone ❑ By Email/Online		Location

97	Name		Date
	❑ In Person ❑ By Phone ❑ By Email/Online		Location
98	Name		Date
	❑ In Person ❑ By Phone ❑ By Email/Online		Location
99	Name		Date
	❑ In Person ❑ By Phone ❑ By Email/Online		Location
100	Name		Date
	❑ In Person ❑ By Phone ❑ By Email/Online		Location

Congratulations!
You are now an Imperial Turtle!

Past Imperial Turtle Degree

101	Name		Date
	❑ In Person ❑ By Phone ❑ By Email/Online		Location
102	Name		Date
	❑ In Person ❑ By Phone ❑ By Email/Online		Location
103	Name		Date
	❑ In Person ❑ By Phone ❑ By Email/Online		Location
104	Name		Date
	❑ In Person ❑ By Phone ❑ By Email/Online		Location
105	Name		Date
	❑ In Person ❑ By Phone ❑ By Email/Online		Location
106	Name		Date
	❑ In Person ❑ By Phone ❑ By Email/Online		Location

107	Name	Date
❑ In Person ❑ By Phone ❑ By Email/Online		Location
108	Name	Date
❑ In Person ❑ By Phone ❑ By Email/Online		Location
109	Name	Date
❑ In Person ❑ By Phone ❑ By Email/Online		Location
110	Name	Date
❑ In Person ❑ By Phone ❑ By Email/Online		Location
111	Name	Date
❑ In Person ❑ By Phone ❑ By Email/Online		Location
112	Name	Date
❑ In Person ❑ By Phone ❑ By Email/Online		Location
113	Name	Date
❑ In Person ❑ By Phone ❑ By Email/Online		Location
114	Name	Date
❑ In Person ❑ By Phone ❑ By Email/Online		Location

115	Name	Date
	❏ In Person ❏ By Phone ❏ By Email/Online	Location
116	Name	Date
	❏ In Person ❏ By Phone ❏ By Email/Online	Location
117	Name	Date
	❏ In Person ❏ By Phone ❏ By Email/Online	Location
118	Name	Date
	❏ In Person ❏ By Phone ❏ By Email/Online	Location
119	Name	Date
	❏ In Person ❏ By Phone ❏ By Email/Online	Location
120	Name	Date
	❏ In Person ❏ By Phone ❏ By Email/Online	Location
121	Name	Date
	❏ In Person ❏ By Phone ❏ By Email/Online	Location
122	Name	Date
	❏ In Person ❏ By Phone ❏ By Email/Online	Location

123	Name		Date
	❑ In Person ❑ By Phone ❑ By Email/Online		Location
124	Name		Date
	❑ In Person ❑ By Phone ❑ By Email/Online		Location
125	Name		Date
	❑ In Person ❑ By Phone ❑ By Email/Online		Location
126	Name		Date
	❑ In Person ❑ By Phone ❑ By Email/Online		Location
127	Name		Date
	❑ In Person ❑ By Phone ❑ By Email/Online		Location
128	Name		Date
	❑ In Person ❑ By Phone ❑ By Email/Online		Location
129	Name		Date
	❑ In Person ❑ By Phone ❑ By Email/Online		Location
130	Name		Date
	❑ In Person ❑ By Phone ❑ By Email/Online		Location

131	Name	Date
	❏ In Person ❏ By Phone ❏ By Email/Online	Location
132	Name	Date
	❏ In Person ❏ By Phone ❏ By Email/Online	Location
133	Name	Date
	❏ In Person ❏ By Phone ❏ By Email/Online	Location
134	Name	Date
	❏ In Person ❏ By Phone ❏ By Email/Online	Location
135	Name	Date
	❏ In Person ❏ By Phone ❏ By Email/Online	Location
136	Name	Date
	❏ In Person ❏ By Phone ❏ By Email/Online	Location
137	Name	Date
	❏ In Person ❏ By Phone ❏ By Email/Online	Location
138	Name	Date
	❏ In Person ❏ By Phone ❏ By Email/Online	Location

139	Name	Date
❑ In Person ❑ By Phone ❑ By Email/Online		Location
140	Name	Date
❑ In Person ❑ By Phone ❑ By Email/Online		Location
141	Name	Date
❑ In Person ❑ By Phone ❑ By Email/Online		Location
142	Name	Date
❑ In Person ❑ By Phone ❑ By Email/Online		Location
143	Name	Date
❑ In Person ❑ By Phone ❑ By Email/Online		Location
144	Name	Date
❑ In Person ❑ By Phone ❑ By Email/Online		Location
145	Name	Date
❑ In Person ❑ By Phone ❑ By Email/Online		Location
146	Name	Date
❑ In Person ❑ By Phone ❑ By Email/Online		Location

147	Name		Date
	❑ In Person ❑ By Phone ❑ By Email/Online		Location
148	Name		Date
	❑ In Person ❑ By Phone ❑ By Email/Online		Location
149	Name		Date
	❑ In Person ❑ By Phone ❑ By Email/Online		Location
150	Name		Date
	❑ In Person ❑ By Phone ❑ By Email/Online		Location

Congratulations!
You are now a Past Imperial Turtle!

Master Imperial Turtle Degree

151	Name		Date
	❏ In Person ❏ By Phone ❏ By Email/Online		Location
152	Name		Date
	❏ In Person ❏ By Phone ❏ By Email/Online		Location
153	Name		Date
	❏ In Person ❏ By Phone ❏ By Email/Online		Location
154	Name		Date
	❏ In Person ❏ By Phone ❏ By Email/Online		Location
155	Name		Date
	❏ In Person ❏ By Phone ❏ By Email/Online		Location
156	Name		Date
	❏ In Person ❏ By Phone ❏ By Email/Online		Location

157	Name	Date
❑ In Person ❑ By Phone ❑ By Email/Online		Location
158	Name	Date
❑ In Person ❑ By Phone ❑ By Email/Online		Location
159	Name	Date
❑ In Person ❑ By Phone ❑ By Email/Online		Location
160	Name	Date
❑ In Person ❑ By Phone ❑ By Email/Online		Location
161	Name	Date
❑ In Person ❑ By Phone ❑ By Email/Online		Location
162	Name	Date
❑ In Person ❑ By Phone ❑ By Email/Online		Location
163	Name	Date
❑ In Person ❑ By Phone ❑ By Email/Online		Location
164	Name	Date
❑ In Person ❑ By Phone ❑ By Email/Online		Location

165	Name	Date
❑ In Person ❑ By Phone ❑ By Email/Online	Location	
166	Name	Date
❑ In Person ❑ By Phone ❑ By Email/Online	Location	
167	Name	Date
❑ In Person ❑ By Phone ❑ By Email/Online	Location	
168	Name	Date
❑ In Person ❑ By Phone ❑ By Email/Online	Location	
169	Name	Date
❑ In Person ❑ By Phone ❑ By Email/Online	Location	
170	Name	Date
❑ In Person ❑ By Phone ❑ By Email/Online	Location	
171	Name	Date
❑ In Person ❑ By Phone ❑ By Email/Online	Location	
172	Name	Date
❑ In Person ❑ By Phone ❑ By Email/Online	Location	

173	Name	Date
	❑ In Person ❑ By Phone ❑ By Email/Online	Location
174	Name	Date
	❑ In Person ❑ By Phone ❑ By Email/Online	Location
175	Name	Date
	❑ In Person ❑ By Phone ❑ By Email/Online	Location
176	Name	Date
	❑ In Person ❑ By Phone ❑ By Email/Online	Location
177	Name	Date
	❑ In Person ❑ By Phone ❑ By Email/Online	Location
178	Name	Date
	❑ In Person ❑ By Phone ❑ By Email/Online	Location
179	Name	Date
	❑ In Person ❑ By Phone ❑ By Email/Online	Location
180	Name	Date
	❑ In Person ❑ By Phone ❑ By Email/Online	Location

181	Name		Date
	❑ In Person ❑ By Phone ❑ By Email/Online		Location
182	Name		Date
	❑ In Person ❑ By Phone ❑ By Email/Online		Location
183	Name		Date
	❑ In Person ❑ By Phone ❑ By Email/Online		Location
184	Name		Date
	❑ In Person ❑ By Phone ❑ By Email/Online		Location
185	Name		Date
	❑ In Person ❑ By Phone ❑ By Email/Online		Location
186	Name		Date
	❑ In Person ❑ By Phone ❑ By Email/Online		Location
187	Name		Date
	❑ In Person ❑ By Phone ❑ By Email/Online		Location
188	Name		Date
	❑ In Person ❑ By Phone ❑ By Email/Online		Location

189	Name	Date
	❑ In Person ❑ By Phone ❑ By Email/Online	Location
190	Name	Date
	❑ In Person ❑ By Phone ❑ By Email/Online	Location
191	Name	Date
	❑ In Person ❑ By Phone ❑ By Email/Online	Location
192	Name	Date
	❑ In Person ❑ By Phone ❑ By Email/Online	Location
193	Name	Date
	❑ In Person ❑ By Phone ❑ By Email/Online	Location
194	Name	Date
	❑ In Person ❑ By Phone ❑ By Email/Online	Location
195	Name	Date
	❑ In Person ❑ By Phone ❑ By Email/Online	Location
196	Name	Date
	❑ In Person ❑ By Phone ❑ By Email/Online	Location

197	Name	Date
	❑ In Person ❑ By Phone ❑ By Email/Online	Location
198	Name	Date
	❑ In Person ❑ By Phone ❑ By Email/Online	Location
199	Name	Date
	❑ In Person ❑ By Phone ❑ By Email/Online	Location
200	Name	Date
	❑ In Person ❑ By Phone ❑ By Email/Online	Location
201	Name	Date
	❑ In Person ❑ By Phone ❑ By Email/Online	Location
202	Name	Date
	❑ In Person ❑ By Phone ❑ By Email/Online	Location
203	Name	Date
	❑ In Person ❑ By Phone ❑ By Email/Online	Location
204	Name	Date
	❑ In Person ❑ By Phone ❑ By Email/Online	Location

205	Name	Date
	❑ In Person ❑ By Phone ❑ By Email/Online	Location
206	Name	Date
	❑ In Person ❑ By Phone ❑ By Email/Online	Location
207	Name	Date
	❑ In Person ❑ By Phone ❑ By Email/Online	Location
208	Name	Date
	❑ In Person ❑ By Phone ❑ By Email/Online	Location
209	Name	Date
	❑ In Person ❑ By Phone ❑ By Email/Online	Location
210	Name	Date
	❑ In Person ❑ By Phone ❑ By Email/Online	Location
211	Name	Date
	❑ In Person ❑ By Phone ❑ By Email/Online	Location
212	Name	Date
	❑ In Person ❑ By Phone ❑ By Email/Online	Location

213	Name	Date
	❑ In Person ❑ By Phone ❑ By Email/Online	Location
214	Name	Date
	❑ In Person ❑ By Phone ❑ By Email/Online	Location
215	Name	Date
	❑ In Person ❑ By Phone ❑ By Email/Online	Location
216	Name	Date
	❑ In Person ❑ By Phone ❑ By Email/Online	Location
217	Name	Date
	❑ In Person ❑ By Phone ❑ By Email/Online	Location
218	Name	Date
	❑ In Person ❑ By Phone ❑ By Email/Online	Location
219	Name	Date
	❑ In Person ❑ By Phone ❑ By Email/Online	Location
220	Name	Date
	❑ In Person ❑ By Phone ❑ By Email/Online	Location

221	Name	Date
	❑ In Person ❑ By Phone ❑ By Email/Online	Location
222	Name	Date
	❑ In Person ❑ By Phone ❑ By Email/Online	Location
223	Name	Date
	❑ In Person ❑ By Phone ❑ By Email/Online	Location
224	Name	Date
	❑ In Person ❑ By Phone ❑ By Email/Online	Location
225	Name	Date
	❑ In Person ❑ By Phone ❑ By Email/Online	Location
226	Name	Date
	❑ In Person ❑ By Phone ❑ By Email/Online	Location
227	Name	Date
	❑ In Person ❑ By Phone ❑ By Email/Online	Location
228	Name	Date
	❑ In Person ❑ By Phone ❑ By Email/Online	Location

229	Name	Date
	☐ In Person ☐ By Phone ☐ By Email/Online	Location
230	Name	Date
	☐ In Person ☐ By Phone ☐ By Email/Online	Location
231	Name	Date
	☐ In Person ☐ By Phone ☐ By Email/Online	Location
232	Name	Date
	☐ In Person ☐ By Phone ☐ By Email/Online	Location
233	Name	Date
	☐ In Person ☐ By Phone ☐ By Email/Online	Location
234	Name	Date
	☐ In Person ☐ By Phone ☐ By Email/Online	Location
235	Name	Date
	☐ In Person ☐ By Phone ☐ By Email/Online	Location
236	Name	Date
	☐ In Person ☐ By Phone ☐ By Email/Online	Location

237	Name	Date
	❑ In Person ❑ By Phone ❑ By Email/Online	Location
238	Name	Date
	❑ In Person ❑ By Phone ❑ By Email/Online	Location
239	Name	Date
	❑ In Person ❑ By Phone ❑ By Email/Online	Location
240	Name	Date
	❑ In Person ❑ By Phone ❑ By Email/Online	Location
241	Name	Date
	❑ In Person ❑ By Phone ❑ By Email/Online	Location
242	Name	Date
	❑ In Person ❑ By Phone ❑ By Email/Online	Location
243	Name	Date
	❑ In Person ❑ By Phone ❑ By Email/Online	Location
244	Name	Date
	❑ In Person ❑ By Phone ❑ By Email/Online	Location

245	Name		Date
	❑ In Person ❑ By Phone ❑ By Email/Online		Location
246	Name		Date
	❑ In Person ❑ By Phone ❑ By Email/Online		Location
247	Name		Date
	❑ In Person ❑ By Phone ❑ By Email/Online		Location
248	Name		Date
	❑ In Person ❑ By Phone ❑ By Email/Online		Location
249	Name		Date
	❑ In Person ❑ By Phone ❑ By Email/Online		Location
250	Name		Date
	❑ In Person ❑ By Phone ❑ By Email/Online		Location
251	Name		Date
	❑ In Person ❑ By Phone ❑ By Email/Online		Location
252	Name		Date
	❑ In Person ❑ By Phone ❑ By Email/Online		Location

253	Name	Date
	❑ In Person ❑ By Phone ❑ By Email/Online	Location
254	Name	Date
	❑ In Person ❑ By Phone ❑ By Email/Online	Location
255	Name	Date
	❑ In Person ❑ By Phone ❑ By Email/Online	Location
256	Name	Date
	❑ In Person ❑ By Phone ❑ By Email/Online	Location
257	Name	Date
	❑ In Person ❑ By Phone ❑ By Email/Online	Location
258	Name	Date
	❑ In Person ❑ By Phone ❑ By Email/Online	Location
259	Name	Date
	❑ In Person ❑ By Phone ❑ By Email/Online	Location
260	Name	Date
	❑ In Person ❑ By Phone ❑ By Email/Online	Location

261	Name	Date
	❏ In Person ❏ By Phone ❏ By Email/Online	Location
262	Name	Date
	❏ In Person ❏ By Phone ❏ By Email/Online	Location
263	Name	Date
	❏ In Person ❏ By Phone ❏ By Email/Online	Location
264	Name	Date
	❏ In Person ❏ By Phone ❏ By Email/Online	Location
265	Name	Date
	❏ In Person ❏ By Phone ❏ By Email/Online	Location
266	Name	Date
	❏ In Person ❏ By Phone ❏ By Email/Online	Location
267	Name	Date
	❏ In Person ❏ By Phone ❏ By Email/Online	Location
268	Name	Date
	❏ In Person ❏ By Phone ❏ By Email/Online	Location

269	Name	Date
	❑ In Person ❑ By Phone ❑ By Email/Online	Location
270	Name	Date
	❑ In Person ❑ By Phone ❑ By Email/Online	Location
271	Name	Date
	❑ In Person ❑ By Phone ❑ By Email/Online	Location
278	Name	Date
	❑ In Person ❑ By Phone ❑ By Email/Online	Location
279	Name	Date
	❑ In Person ❑ By Phone ❑ By Email/Online	Location
280	Name	Date
	❑ In Person ❑ By Phone ❑ By Email/Online	Location
281	Name	Date
	❑ In Person ❑ By Phone ❑ By Email/Online	Location
282	Name	Date
	❑ In Person ❑ By Phone ❑ By Email/Online	Location

283	Name		Date
	❑ In Person ❑ By Phone ❑ By Email/Online		Location
284	Name		Date
	❑ In Person ❑ By Phone ❑ By Email/Online		Location
285	Name		Date
	❑ In Person ❑ By Phone ❑ By Email/Online		Location
286	Name		Date
	❑ In Person ❑ By Phone ❑ By Email/Online		Location
287	Name		Date
	❑ In Person ❑ By Phone ❑ By Email/Online		Location
288	Name		Date
	❑ In Person ❑ By Phone ❑ By Email/Online		Location
289	Name		Date
	❑ In Person ❑ By Phone ❑ By Email/Online		Location
290	Name		Date
	❑ In Person ❑ By Phone ❑ By Email/Online		Location

291	Name	Date
	❑ In Person ❑ By Phone ❑ By Email/Online	Location
292	Name	Date
	❑ In Person ❑ By Phone ❑ By Email/Online	Location
293	Name	Date
	❑ In Person ❑ By Phone ❑ By Email/Online	Location
294	Name	Date
	❑ In Person ❑ By Phone ❑ By Email/Online	Location
295	Name	Date
	❑ In Person ❑ By Phone ❑ By Email/Online	Location
296	Name	Date
	❑ In Person ❑ By Phone ❑ By Email/Online	Location
297	Name	Date
	❑ In Person ❑ By Phone ❑ By Email/Online	Location
298	Name	Date
	❑ In Person ❑ By Phone ❑ By Email/Online	Location

299	Name		Date
	❑ In Person ❑ By Phone ❑ By Email/Online		Location
300	Name		Date
	❑ In Person ❑ By Phone ❑ By Email/Online		Location
301	Name		Date
	❑ In Person ❑ By Phone ❑ By Email/Online		Location
302	Name		Date
	❑ In Person ❑ By Phone ❑ By Email/Online		Location
303	Name		Date
	❑ In Person ❑ By Phone ❑ By Email/Online		Location
304	Name		Date
	❑ In Person ❑ By Phone ❑ By Email/Online		Location
305	Name		Date
	❑ In Person ❑ By Phone ❑ By Email/Online		Location
306	Name		Date
	❑ In Person ❑ By Phone ❑ By Email/Online		Location

307	Name	Date
	☐ In Person ☐ By Phone ☐ By Email/Online	Location
308	Name	Date
	☐ In Person ☐ By Phone ☐ By Email/Online	Location
309	Name	Date
	☐ In Person ☐ By Phone ☐ By Email/Online	Location
310	Name	Date
	☐ In Person ☐ By Phone ☐ By Email/Online	Location
311	Name	Date
	☐ In Person ☐ By Phone ☐ By Email/Online	Location
312	Name	Date
	☐ In Person ☐ By Phone ☐ By Email/Online	Location
313	Name	Date
	☐ In Person ☐ By Phone ☐ By Email/Online	Location
314	Name	Date
	☐ In Person ☐ By Phone ☐ By Email/Online	Location

315	Name	Date
	❑ In Person ❑ By Phone ❑ By Email/Online	Location
316	Name	Date
	❑ In Person ❑ By Phone ❑ By Email/Online	Location
317	Name	Date
	❑ In Person ❑ By Phone ❑ By Email/Online	Location
318	Name	Date
	❑ In Person ❑ By Phone ❑ By Email/Online	Location
319	Name	Date
	❑ In Person ❑ By Phone ❑ By Email/Online	Location
320	Name	Date
	❑ In Person ❑ By Phone ❑ By Email/Online	Location
321	Name	Date
	❑ In Person ❑ By Phone ❑ By Email/Online	Location
322	Name	Date
	❑ In Person ❑ By Phone ❑ By Email/Online	Location

323	Name	Date
	❑ In Person ❑ By Phone ❑ By Email/Online	Location
324	Name	Date
	❑ In Person ❑ By Phone ❑ By Email/Online	Location
325	Name	Date
	❑ In Person ❑ By Phone ❑ By Email/Online	Location
326	Name	Date
	❑ In Person ❑ By Phone ❑ By Email/Online	Location
327	Name	Date
	❑ In Person ❑ By Phone ❑ By Email/Online	Location
328	Name	Date
	❑ In Person ❑ By Phone ❑ By Email/Online	Location
329	Name	Date
	❑ In Person ❑ By Phone ❑ By Email/Online	Location
330	Name	Date
	❑ In Person ❑ By Phone ❑ By Email/Online	Location

331	Name		Date
	❑ In Person ❑ By Phone ❑ By Email/Online		Location
332	Name		Date
	❑ In Person ❑ By Phone ❑ By Email/Online		Location
333	Name		Date
	❑ In Person ❑ By Phone ❑ By Email/Online		Location
334	Name		Date
	❑ In Person ❑ By Phone ❑ By Email/Online		Location
335	Name		Date
	❑ In Person ❑ By Phone ❑ By Email/Online		Location
336	Name		Date
	❑ In Person ❑ By Phone ❑ By Email/Online		Location
337	Name		Date
	❑ In Person ❑ By Phone ❑ By Email/Online		Location
338	Name		Date
	❑ In Person ❑ By Phone ❑ By Email/Online		Location

339	Name	Date
	❏ In Person ❏ By Phone ❏ By Email/Online	Location
340	Name	Date
	❏ In Person ❏ By Phone ❏ By Email/Online	Location
341	Name	Date
	❏ In Person ❏ By Phone ❏ By Email/Online	Location
342	Name	Date
	❏ In Person ❏ By Phone ❏ By Email/Online	Location
343	Name	Date
	❏ In Person ❏ By Phone ❏ By Email/Online	Location
344	Name	Date
	❏ In Person ❏ By Phone ❏ By Email/Online	Location
345	Name	Date
	❏ In Person ❏ By Phone ❏ By Email/Online	Location
346	Name	Date
	❏ In Person ❏ By Phone ❏ By Email/Online	Location

347	Name	Date
❑ In Person ❑ By Phone ❑ By Email/Online		Location
348	Name	Date
❑ In Person ❑ By Phone ❑ By Email/Online		Location
349	Name	Date
❑ In Person ❑ By Phone ❑ By Email/Online		Location
350	Name	Date
❑ In Person ❑ By Phone ❑ By Email/Online		Location
351	Name	Date
❑ In Person ❑ By Phone ❑ By Email/Online		Location
352	Name	Date
❑ In Person ❑ By Phone ❑ By Email/Online		Location
353	Name	Date
❑ In Person ❑ By Phone ❑ By Email/Online		Location
354	Name	Date
❑ In Person ❑ By Phone ❑ By Email/Online		Location

355	Name	Date
	❏ In Person ❏ By Phone ❏ By Email/Online	Location
356	Name	Date
	❏ In Person ❏ By Phone ❏ By Email/Online	Location
357	Name	Date
	❏ In Person ❏ By Phone ❏ By Email/Online	Location
358	Name	Date
	❏ In Person ❏ By Phone ❏ By Email/Online	Location
359	Name	Date
	❏ In Person ❏ By Phone ❏ By Email/Online	Location
360	Name	Date
	❏ In Person ❏ By Phone ❏ By Email/Online	Location
361	Name	Date
	❏ In Person ❏ By Phone ❏ By Email/Online	Location
362	Name	Date
	❏ In Person ❏ By Phone ❏ By Email/Online	Location

363	Name		Date
	❏ In Person ❏ By Phone ❏ By Email/Online		Location
364	Name		Date
	❏ In Person ❏ By Phone ❏ By Email/Online		Location
365	Name		Date
	❏ In Person ❏ By Phone ❏ By Email/Online		Location
366	Name		Date
	❏ In Person ❏ By Phone ❏ By Email/Online		Location
367	Name		Date
	❏ In Person ❏ By Phone ❏ By Email/Online		Location
368	Name		Date
	❏ In Person ❏ By Phone ❏ By Email/Online		Location
369	Name		Date
	❏ In Person ❏ By Phone ❏ By Email/Online		Location
370	Name		Date
	❏ In Person ❏ By Phone ❏ By Email/Online		Location

371	Name	Date
	❑ In Person ❑ By Phone ❑ By Email/Online	Location
372	Name	Date
	❑ In Person ❑ By Phone ❑ By Email/Online	Location
373	Name	Date
	❑ In Person ❑ By Phone ❑ By Email/Online	Location
374	Name	Date
	❑ In Person ❑ By Phone ❑ By Email/Online	Location
375	Name	Date
	❑ In Person ❑ By Phone ❑ By Email/Online	Location
376	Name	Date
	❑ In Person ❑ By Phone ❑ By Email/Online	Location
377	Name	Date
	❑ In Person ❑ By Phone ❑ By Email/Online	Location
378	Name	Date
	❑ In Person ❑ By Phone ❑ By Email/Online	Location

379	Name	Date
	❑ In Person ❑ By Phone ❑ By Email/Online	Location
380	Name	Date
	❑ In Person ❑ By Phone ❑ By Email/Online	Location
381	Name	Date
	❑ In Person ❑ By Phone ❑ By Email/Online	Location
382	Name	Date
	❑ In Person ❑ By Phone ❑ By Email/Online	Location
383	Name	Date
	❑ In Person ❑ By Phone ❑ By Email/Online	Location
384	Name	Date
	❑ In Person ❑ By Phone ❑ By Email/Online	Location
385	Name	Date
	❑ In Person ❑ By Phone ❑ By Email/Online	Location
386	Name	Date
	❑ In Person ❑ By Phone ❑ By Email/Online	Location

387	Name	Date
	❑ In Person ❑ By Phone ❑ By Email/Online	Location
388	Name	Date
	❑ In Person ❑ By Phone ❑ By Email/Online	Location
389	Name	Date
	❑ In Person ❑ By Phone ❑ By Email/Online	Location
390	Name	Date
	❑ In Person ❑ By Phone ❑ By Email/Online	Location
391	Name	Date
	❑ In Person ❑ By Phone ❑ By Email/Online	Location
392	Name	Date
	❑ In Person ❑ By Phone ❑ By Email/Online	Location
393	Name	Date
	❑ In Person ❑ By Phone ❑ By Email/Online	Location
394	Name	Date
	❑ In Person ❑ By Phone ❑ By Email/Online	Location

395	Name		Date
	❑ In Person ❑ By Phone ❑ By Email/Online		Location
396	Name		Date
	❑ In Person ❑ By Phone ❑ By Email/Online		Location
397	Name		Date
	❑ In Person ❑ By Phone ❑ By Email/Online		Location
398	Name		Date
	❑ In Person ❑ By Phone ❑ By Email/Online		Location
399	Name		Date
	❑ In Person ❑ By Phone ❑ By Email/Online		Location
400	Name		Date
	❑ In Person ❑ By Phone ❑ By Email/Online		Location
401	Name		Date
	❑ In Person ❑ By Phone ❑ By Email/Online		Location
402	Name		Date
	❑ In Person ❑ By Phone ❑ By Email/Online		Location

403	Name	Date
	❑ In Person ❑ By Phone ❑ By Email/Online	Location
404	Name	Date
	❑ In Person ❑ By Phone ❑ By Email/Online	Location
405	Name	Date
	❑ In Person ❑ By Phone ❑ By Email/Online	Location
406	Name	Date
	❑ In Person ❑ By Phone ❑ By Email/Online	Location
407	Name	Date
	❑ In Person ❑ By Phone ❑ By Email/Online	Location
408	Name	Date
	❑ In Person ❑ By Phone ❑ By Email/Online	Location
409	Name	Date
	❑ In Person ❑ By Phone ❑ By Email/Online	Location
410	Name	Date
	❑ In Person ❑ By Phone ❑ By Email/Online	Location

411	Name		Date
	❑ In Person ❑ By Phone ❑ By Email/Online		Location
412	Name		Date
	❑ In Person ❑ By Phone ❑ By Email/Online		Location
413	Name		Date
	❑ In Person ❑ By Phone ❑ By Email/Online		Location
414	Name		Date
	❑ In Person ❑ By Phone ❑ By Email/Online		Location
415	Name		Date
	❑ In Person ❑ By Phone ❑ By Email/Online		Location
416	Name		Date
	❑ In Person ❑ By Phone ❑ By Email/Online		Location
417	Name		Date
	❑ In Person ❑ By Phone ❑ By Email/Online		Location
418	Name		Date
	❑ In Person ❑ By Phone ❑ By Email/Online		Location

419	Name		Date
	❑ In Person ❑ By Phone ❑ By Email/Online		Location
420	Name		Date
	❑ In Person ❑ By Phone ❑ By Email/Online		Location
421	Name		Date
	❑ In Person ❑ By Phone ❑ By Email/Online		Location
422	Name		Date
	❑ In Person ❑ By Phone ❑ By Email/Online		Location
423	Name		Date
	❑ In Person ❑ By Phone ❑ By Email/Online		Location
424	Name		Date
	❑ In Person ❑ By Phone ❑ By Email/Online		Location
425	Name		Date
	❑ In Person ❑ By Phone ❑ By Email/Online		Location
426	Name		Date
	❑ In Person ❑ By Phone ❑ By Email/Online		Location

427	Name	Date
	❑ In Person ❑ By Phone ❑ By Email/Online	Location
428	Name	Date
	❑ In Person ❑ By Phone ❑ By Email/Online	Location
429	Name	Date
	❑ In Person ❑ By Phone ❑ By Email/Online	Location
430	Name	Date
	❑ In Person ❑ By Phone ❑ By Email/Online	Location
431	Name	Date
	❑ In Person ❑ By Phone ❑ By Email/Online	Location
432	Name	Date
	❑ In Person ❑ By Phone ❑ By Email/Online	Location
433	Name	Date
	❑ In Person ❑ By Phone ❑ By Email/Online	Location
434	Name	Date
	❑ In Person ❑ By Phone ❑ By Email/Online	Location

435	Name		Date
	❑ In Person ❑ By Phone ❑ By Email/Online		Location
436	Name		Date
	❑ In Person ❑ By Phone ❑ By Email/Online		Location
437	Name		Date
	❑ In Person ❑ By Phone ❑ By Email/Online		Location
438	Name		Date
	❑ In Person ❑ By Phone ❑ By Email/Online		Location
439	Name		Date
	❑ In Person ❑ By Phone ❑ By Email/Online		Location
440	Name		Date
	❑ In Person ❑ By Phone ❑ By Email/Online		Location
441	Name		Date
	❑ In Person ❑ By Phone ❑ By Email/Online		Location
442	Name		Date
	❑ In Person ❑ By Phone ❑ By Email/Online		Location

443	Name		Date
	❑ In Person ❑ By Phone ❑ By Email/Online		Location
444	Name		Date
	❑ In Person ❑ By Phone ❑ By Email/Online		Location
445	Name		Date
	❑ In Person ❑ By Phone ❑ By Email/Online		Location
446	Name		Date
	❑ In Person ❑ By Phone ❑ By Email/Online		Location
447	Name		Date
	❑ In Person ❑ By Phone ❑ By Email/Online		Location
448	Name		Date
	❑ In Person ❑ By Phone ❑ By Email/Online		Location
449	Name		Date
	❑ In Person ❑ By Phone ❑ By Email/Online		Location
450	Name		Date
	❑ In Person ❑ By Phone ❑ By Email/Online		Location

451	Name	Date
	❑ In Person ❑ By Phone ❑ By Email/Online	Location
452	Name	Date
	❑ In Person ❑ By Phone ❑ By Email/Online	Location
453	Name	Date
	❑ In Person ❑ By Phone ❑ By Email/Online	Location
454	Name	Date
	❑ In Person ❑ By Phone ❑ By Email/Online	Location
455	Name	Date
	❑ In Person ❑ By Phone ❑ By Email/Online	Location
456	Name	Date
	❑ In Person ❑ By Phone ❑ By Email/Online	Location
457	Name	Date
	❑ In Person ❑ By Phone ❑ By Email/Online	Location
458	Name	Date
	❑ In Person ❑ By Phone ❑ By Email/Online	Location

	Name	Date
459		
	❑ In Person ❑ By Phone ❑ By Email/Online	Location
460	Name	Date
	❑ In Person ❑ By Phone ❑ By Email/Online	Location
461	Name	Date
	❑ In Person ❑ By Phone ❑ By Email/Online	Location
462	Name	Date
	❑ In Person ❑ By Phone ❑ By Email/Online	Location
463	Name	Date
	❑ In Person ❑ By Phone ❑ By Email/Online	Location
464	Name	Date
	❑ In Person ❑ By Phone ❑ By Email/Online	Location
465	Name	Date
	❑ In Person ❑ By Phone ❑ By Email/Online	Location
466	Name	Date
	❑ In Person ❑ By Phone ❑ By Email/Online	Location

467	Name	Date
	❏ In Person ❏ By Phone ❏ By Email/Online	Location
468	Name	Date
	❏ In Person ❏ By Phone ❏ By Email/Online	Location
469	Name	Date
	❏ In Person ❏ By Phone ❏ By Email/Online	Location
470	Name	Date
	❏ In Person ❏ By Phone ❏ By Email/Online	Location
471	Name	Date
	❏ In Person ❏ By Phone ❏ By Email/Online	Location
472	Name	Date
	❏ In Person ❏ By Phone ❏ By Email/Online	Location
473	Name	Date
	❏ In Person ❏ By Phone ❏ By Email/Online	Location
474	Name	Date
	❏ In Person ❏ By Phone ❏ By Email/Online	Location

475	Name	Date
❏ In Person ❏ By Phone ❏ By Email/Online	Location	
476	Name	Date
❏ In Person ❏ By Phone ❏ By Email/Online	Location	
478	Name	Date
❏ In Person ❏ By Phone ❏ By Email/Online	Location	
479	Name	Date
❏ In Person ❏ By Phone ❏ By Email/Online	Location	
480	Name	Date
❏ In Person ❏ By Phone ❏ By Email/Online	Location	
481	Name	Date
❏ In Person ❏ By Phone ❏ By Email/Online	Location	
482	Name	Date
❏ In Person ❏ By Phone ❏ By Email/Online	Location	
483	Name	Date
❏ In Person ❏ By Phone ❏ By Email/Online	Location	

484	Name	Date
	❏ In Person ❏ By Phone ❏ By Email/Online	Location
485	Name	Date
	❏ In Person ❏ By Phone ❏ By Email/Online	Location
486	Name	Date
	❏ In Person ❏ By Phone ❏ By Email/Online	Location
487	Name	Date
	❏ In Person ❏ By Phone ❏ By Email/Online	Location
488	Name	Date
	❏ In Person ❏ By Phone ❏ By Email/Online	Location
489	Name	Date
	❏ In Person ❏ By Phone ❏ By Email/Online	Location
490	Name	Date
	❏ In Person ❏ By Phone ❏ By Email/Online	Location
491	Name	Date
	❏ In Person ❏ By Phone ❏ By Email/Online	Location

492	Name		Date
	❑ In Person ❑ By Phone ❑ By Email/Online		Location
493	Name		Date
	❑ In Person ❑ By Phone ❑ By Email/Online		Location
494	Name		Date
	❑ In Person ❑ By Phone ❑ By Email/Online		Location
495	Name		Date
	❑ In Person ❑ By Phone ❑ By Email/Online		Location
496	Name		Date
	❑ In Person ❑ By Phone ❑ By Email/Online		Location
497	Name		Date
	❑ In Person ❑ By Phone ❑ By Email/Online		Location
498	Name		Date
	❑ In Person ❑ By Phone ❑ By Email/Online		Location
499	Name		Date
	❑ In Person ❑ By Phone ❑ By Email/Online		Location

500	Name		Date
	❑ In Person ❑ By Phone ❑ By Email/Online		Location

Congratulations!

Now, after years, You are a

MASTER IMPERIAL TURTLE!

5 POND AFFILIATIONS

As a Turtle in Good Standing, I have been affiliated with and/or helped start the following Ponds (Chapters):

Pond Name	
Pond Location or Web Address (if online group)	
Sponsoring Organization (if any)	
Date Entered the Pond	Date Left the Pond
Charter Member? ❑ YES ❑ NO	Date Pond Discovered (Chartered)

Pond Name	
Pond Location or Web Address (if online group)	
Sponsoring Organization (if any)	
Date Entered the Pond	Date Left the Pond
Charter Member? ❑ YES ❑ NO	Date Pond Discovered (Chartered)

Pond Name	
Pond Location or Web Address (if online group)	
Sponsoring Organization (if any)	
Date Entered the Pond	Date Left the Pond
Charter Member? ❑ YES ❑ NO	Date Pond Discovered (Chartered)

Pond Name	
Pond Location or Web Address (if online group)	
Sponsoring Organization (if any)	
Date Entered the Pond	Date Left the Pond
Charter Member? ❑ YES ❑ NO	Date Pond Discovered (Chartered)

Pond Name	
Pond Location or Web Address (if online group)	
Sponsoring Organization (if any)	
Date Entered the Pond	Date Left the Pond
Charter Member? ❑ YES ❑ NO	Date Pond Discovered (Chartered)

Pond Name	
Pond Location or Web Address (if online group)	
Sponsoring Organization (if any)	
Date Entered the Pond	Date Left the Pond
Charter Member? ❏ YES ❏ NO	Date Pond Discovered (Chartered)

Pond Name	
Pond Location or Web Address (if online group)	
Sponsoring Organization (if any)	
Date Entered the Pond	Date Left the Pond
Charter Member? ❏ YES ❏ NO	Date Pond Discovered (Chartered)

Pond Name	
Pond Location or Web Address (if online group)	
Sponsoring Organization (if any)	
Date Entered the Pond	Date Left the Pond
Charter Member?　❑ YES　❑ NO	Date Pond Discovered (Chartered)

Pond Name	
Pond Location or Web Address (if online group)	
Sponsoring Organization (if any)	
Date Entered the Pond	Date Left the Pond
Charter Member?　❑ YES　❑ NO	Date Pond Discovered (Chartered)

Pond Name	
Pond Location or Web Address (if online group)	
Sponsoring Organization (if any)	
Date Entered the Pond	Date Left the Pond
Charter Member? ❏ YES ❏ NO	Date Pond Discovered (Chartered)

Pond Name	
Pond Location or Web Address (if online group)	
Sponsoring Organization (if any)	
Date Entered the Pond	Date Left the Pond
Charter Member? ❏ YES ❏ NO	Date Pond Discovered (Chartered)

ABOUT THE AUTHOR

The Author is a Turtle.

R U A Turtle?

If you ARE NOT,
and you want to become a free Lifetime
Member of this sublime and surreal
Order of Ancient and Honorable Turtles,
then visit the Author on his Turtle Page at:

masonicpress.com

If you ARE a Turtle,

Go forth, be fruitful and multiply!

www.ingramcontent.com/pod-product-compliance
Lightning Source LLC
Chambersburg PA
CBHW060425290526
45791CB00002B/869